S0-CBK-835

LAURA STORTONI

The Moon and the Island

Introduction

by

Diane di Prima

Copyright © Hesperia Press, 1997

Copyright © Laura Stortoni, 1997.

ALL RIGHTS RESERVED. No part of this publication may be reproduced, stored in a retrieval system, or transmitted, in any form or by any means, electronic, mechanical, photocopying, recording or otherwise, without prior permission of Hesperia Press.

Library of Congress Cataloging-in-Publication Data

Stortoni, Laura
The Moon and the Island

Introduction by Diane di Prima.
Includes biographical and bibliographical references and index.
First Edition.

ISBN 0-9641003-3-9

Library of Congress Catalog Card Number: 97-74674

Some of the poems in this volume have been previously published in *Voices in Italian Americana, The Midwest Quarterly, Italian-Americana, Women's Quarterly, Blue Unicorn, The City Lights Review, Koroné, Women's Voices, Gradiva, Rocky Mountain Review, Poetry of the New Immigrants, The Paterson Literary Review, Rain City Review,* and others.

Typography: Harvest Graphics, San Francisco
Cover Design: Doug Mortensen
Printed in the United States of America.

HESPERIA PRESS BOOKS can be ordered through SMALL PRESS DISTRIBUTION, 1341 Seventh Street, Berkeley, CA 94710 (Phone: 510 524-1668; Fax: 510 524-0852), or directly from HESPERIA PRESS, P.O. Box 9246, Berkeley, CA 94709 (Phone: 510 644-8259; Fax: 510 644-2109).

To the memory

of

my father

Renato Stortoni

who called me Laura

because he loved Petrarch

and taught me to love poetry

ABOUT THE POET

An Italian native, Laura Stortoni (a.k.a. Laura Anna Stortoni) was brought up in Milan and received an international education in France, Spain, England and in the United States. She holds higher education degrees and is a Ph.D. Candidate in Comparative Literature at the University of California at Berkeley, specializing in Italian Renaissance. She has taught at major institutions in Oregon and in Northern California, and presently makes her home in Berkeley, California, and in Milan, Italy.

She has published her poetry and poetry translations in *The City Lights Review, The Blue Unicorn, The San Marcos Review, The Midwest Quarterly, Women's Voices, Voices in Italian Americana, The Rocky Mountain Review, Koronè, Italian Americana, The Paterson Literary Review,* and many other publications.

She has co-authored with Mary Prentice Lillie two books of verse translations of Italian Renaissance women poets, *Gaspara Stampa: Selected Poems* (New York: Italica Press, 1994) and *Women Poets of the Italian Renaissance: Courtly Ladies and Courtesans* (New York: Italica Press, 1997).

Sentry Towers, Stortoni's poetry translation of the most recent poetry book by Maria Luisa Spaziani (Italy's candidate for the Nobel Prize for Literature) appeared in July 1996 (Berkeley: Hesperia Press) in dual language edition, and Giuseppe Conte's *The Ocean and the Boy,* with an introduction by Italo Calvino, was published in June of 1997, in dual language edition, also with Hesperia Press.

Stortoni, who writes both in Italian and English, has also translated into Italian and published in Italy poetry by modern American poets, among whom Lawrence Ferlinghetti, John Wieners and Diane di Prima.

CONTENTS

INTRODUCTION

In Laura Stortoni's poems there is the slightly crusty taste of salt, the sea wind on our lips. There is Mediterranean light and Berkeley light and the long spaces of ancient days close as our skin. Laura's work makes bridges. Her world extends from primordial time to the present moment, as her life has literally spanned the old world and the new: it is all palpable and in focus.

Sometimes we are not sure if the world she describes is distant in time or in place: she inhabits the past as the present, the imaginal as the real. Figures from myth, Artemis and Persephone, could be her neighbors, her woman-friends she spoke to just this morning. She simply passes on their messages.

Born in Sicily, raised in Milan, and living more than twenty years in the Bay Area, she spans oceans and continents. Her poem "A Borrowed Tongue" addresses this dilemma, the eternal dilemma of the voyager with two homes, two languages. It is one of the basic dilemmas of America, the confluence of the "old world" and the "new". In Laura Stortoni's work, for instance in "Montezuma Sends Messengers to Cortés," it is hard to say which is "the old world": they are simultaneous, and simultaneously inhabited.

These poems are passionate and sensual, filled with the colors of shells, of red geraniums, the scent of nasturtiums, the sweep of sea and sky, the eyes of children. They are the record of a life lived fiercely and fully. There is here the cry of the wounded and the song of Atalanta from the top of a Burmese temple. There is the shout of love and the bitterness of "relationship" so-called. There is laughter, the shadow of the fig tree, the "cities of light and shadow." The work is variously a poetics of loss and a song of celebration.

John Keats once said of the poet that (s)he should be able to enter the life of other beings: "If a sparrow come before my Window, I take part in its existence and pick about in the gravel." Laura Stortoni has this gift. In her re-adapted translations she speaks in the voice of

Sappho, of Basho or the pre-Socratics. In her own poetry we hear Cassandra faced with the Gulf War, and Penelope dealing with modern infidelity. Her work takes us inside a spiraling bee, the taste of coffee, the colors and sounds of Venice.

In speaking the truth of her own life, this poet changes and reverses our inner landscape. What we held at a distance she brings near, and she gives the immediate a new, longer perspective. She reveals the heroic, questing quality of our own daily lives – makes us literally recognize and own it in ourselves – while at the same time she shows us the domesticity, the nearness, of remote and classical worlds.

As we read we join her in this adventure, this bridging of time and space, one foot in the distant world of our ancestors, one upon "the westward drifting continent," we, too, set out. . .

—Diane di Prima
San Francisco, 1995

I

AS THE BEE EMERGES

But now I think that there is no unreturned love,
the pay is certain one way or another,
(I loved a certain person ardently and my love was not
*   returned,*
Yet out of that I have written these songs).

Walt Whitman

A Borrowed Tongue

Who is poorer than I am?
I can only speak with a borrowed tongue.
Words
garble in my throat and die
drowned in the sweetness
of my native sounds.

Foreign woman, foreign woman,
I love you and I hate you.
When you make me suffer
I must borrow your tongue to cry out.

Who is poorer than I am?
Some people borrow houses
for a roof over their heads.
Some borrow a car
to get from one place to another.
Some borrow a cup of sugar,
company in loneliness.
      Some borrow a book.
      Some borrow a person.
Neither will ever return.

But the poorest of them all
is she who must borrow a tongue.

Jealousy

A chunky
still uncracked
avocado pit
precariously suspended
by three toothpicks
from the rim of a jigger

—unknown feminine hands
placed it on the windowsill—

tells me
it's no longer my kitchen

The First Thanksgiving after a Divorce

This Thanksgiving
I'll carve my own turkey
presiding—five foot two—over my own banquet.
I'll stuff the bird
like the previous years
with chestnuts and apples, raisins, and other goodies.
It'll take seven or eight
precious hours of fussing
by the oven door.

It will be
my own symposium: my blue Wedgwood
and the family silver scintillating
on the embroidered cloth.
Maybe I'll even
have a centerpiece
of fresh flowers, yellow roses, or something
as corny as that.
When the meal is ready
I'll be beautiful—just for myself—

I'll carve the bird I cooked, something
I'd always wanted to do. I'll give myself
both drumsticks, and I'll talk
to the empty chairs.
The chairs were filled with sundry
buttocks at previous banquets.
But no one listened to me anyway.

I'll ask myself: "Would you like a second
helping of creamed onions?" I'll politely
turn myself down. "They are delicious, but . . .
I must watch my weight . . ."

At the end, like my old guests, I'll leave
the mess on the table, and sink into an armchair
by the fireplace.

For dessert I'll have
a piece of Vivaldi.

The Agave

There are plants
that die in blooming

I saw an agave
with its bright flower

at the peak of its stalk

The plant was dying—
Its vigor
flowing

to the aloof flower
up there

proud
unaware

of sickly leaves
stretching like withered arms

towards that glorious

pinnacle

to then fold up
and die

Only an Ocean

We are two children
crying in the dark
separated by the waters
of an ocean and hurt feelings.

In sleep
sometimes
our arms reach out
to find the other's reassuring shape
where it used to be

but now they find the obstruction
of a cold wall.

Only in sleep
could our hands touch again,
for pride
also sleeps. In sleep
reconciling is possible.

But we are
in different hemispheres.
When your hand
looks for mine under the blanket
in the night
of your side of the world,

I'm walking in an Italian market
stunned by the bright colors
of Autumn apples.

The Moon Has Set . . .

Inspired by a fragment by Sappho

The moon has set. So
have the Pleiades. It is midnight.
The hour passes and I
alone lie on my tormented bed.

I remember one night
when the silvery queen
with her last paling rays
lit our entangled bodies.

But a night ran quickly
after another night.
They added up in memory:
they are as countless as stars in the sky.

So, my heart, quietly sleep.
Forget the moon.
Forget our tangled bodies.

Night Time Phone Calls

The night your mother died . . . ah, that dreadful insistent
long distance ring into the dark!
You looked at me with haggard
eyes, mumbled something—
turned around and went back to sleep. I lay awake
crying quietly. You chose
to find comfort in sleep
rather than in my arms. My arms
ached to surround your body with tenderness. My hands
wanted to press your head to my breasts. We had
that in common, among other things, she and I,
firm, motherly breasts.
But my hands lay at the side of my body—
the ephemeral quiet of few hours' sleep
more comforting to you.

That night
I knew it was all over . . .
I sobbed quietly not to shake the bed, not to recall
your pain back to consciousness.
Your shoulders turned against mine—
you slept . . . not to show me your wound.
What had I done
that you should fear I'd choose that night
to rub salt into it?

The morning after. Matter of fact. A solid breakfast.
Plane reservations. I packed. You called a few friends.
We did not talk about <u>her</u>.

Years have gone by. Still, when I hear
the shrill sound of the phone in the night
I remember that night . . . wonder how trust can dissolve
while love is still alive,
leaving
on the stiff skeleton of a marriage
a few shreds of withered
and decomposed flesh.

Ex-Spouses

Now like
two apprentice acrobats
we swing
from a trapeze
counting seconds
at a different rhythm

never meeting in the air

bewildered upside-down faces
in spaces
where our hands used to interlock

When I move forward
I see you move back

Your contour blurs

while I
stretch out my hands
in vain

We've lost timing

Love gives precision
to intuition

Now we are two fools
hanging from our feet
in a topsy-turvy world

But we hold it against each other—
the lack of courage

to leap first

Leaping
may be dying

Ex-Spouses Meet at the Local Supermarket

You're fine. I'm fine
Thats nice and how's your
1)mother/2)father/3)brother?
Hope you're
having a
good time
Im too 'fcourse
Don't imagine
otherwise!
I wouldntwantyoutothink*Imnot*
And you?
Me? Never felt
better!

Burmese Recollections

Squatting by the golden pinnacle of That Byinnyu
I gaze at the whitewashed splendor of Ananda
miles away across the tidal jungle
engulfing the five thousand pagodas of Pagan—
crushing desecrated stupas with its green tentacles.
Beyond it
flows the vast Irrawaddy
                              green on green.

The monks chant:
"Irrawaddy, Irrawaddy,
I'll walk ten thousand miles to drown in your green embrace."

> *Outside the temple hall, Maung Taya, the guide,*
> *patiently waits, chewing betel leaf,*
> *leaning on the hot metal siding of his beat-up jeep,*
> *his checkered silk longyi unaffected by sweat,*
> *though it's the monsoon month of Wagaung,*
> *and who but a crazy foreigner — and a woman at that —*
> *would climb from terrace to terrace,*
> *from passageway to passageway,*
> *the soles of her bare feet (she made no objections*
> *at leaving her sandals at the Gate, as prescribed)*
> *scalded by the burning stone. Maung Taya*
> *shakes his head, as he watches her climb*
> *like a mad goat.*
> *She disappears, then reappears,*
> *then disappears again, then, lo!*
> *She is a dot next to the golden pinnacle.*

I was that woman.

In the chiaroscuro
of the cavernous hall filled with a ceiling-high
expressionless Buddha,
I, who had always been left behind,
started to run ahead of you, away from you,
while clouds of dark wings,
stirred by the echo of footsteps,

fluttered about in terror, to find asylum
behind the statue's gigantic nape.

I now took joy
in playing hide 'n' seek,
hiding my small body in slices of dark shadows,
laughing in silence
at your feet more squeamish than mine,
trying to find clear pathways on the ground
littered with balls of petrified bat excrement,
laughing at your body, too tall, too big
for passageways designed
for the small frames of Burmese monks.

I climb higher than the highest palm tree. A boy,
semi-naked, hidden in a fan of feathery branches,
stares at me in amazement across the void.
A group has now gathered
in front of the deserted
holy That Byinnyu. I spot the orange-colored gauze
of a monk's tunic.

I have left you
and the whole world behind.
Now I am alone,
inebriated
by the power of my strong thighs.

I suddenly feel your loneliness. Where are you?
You could not follow your goat-woman in her crazed ascent,
swift Atalanta reborn, bare-footed devouring the slopes
of her native Mediterranean island.

I descend quickly, dangerously, jumping
from stone to stone, from terrace to terrace.
My heart is pounding.
I am afraid I'll find no one down there.
When I emerge from the first level,
my eyes wince at the blinding sun;
then I discern, like in a negative
the outline of your tall body, stooping over, as if casually
to talk to Maung Taya. You do not turn
to look at me.

A young girl
with blood red lipstick making her mouth like a wound,
comes forward,
with a graceful gesture
offers me a mango, and asks me a question.
Maung Taya, deadpan,
translates: "Why?"
I do not answer. *It's a long story.*
I do not know what to do
with the mango. My stomach
feels queasy.

Now
I am like a small *stupa* in the jungle—
cherishing a modest treasure
within my conic shape.

Lullaby and Requiem to an Unfertilized Egg

Sarcastic
the full moon smiles
through the windowpane.

It's a dark moon, a Saracen
moon. She laughs
a wide laugh.

The egg has dropped
inperceptibly almost
inside me   down the chute.

I've learned
to recognize that signal—
      so many years
         of listening—
But what can I do? I feel
like a poverty-stricken mother
unable to feed her baby.

What desolation
deeper than tonight's! You, little egg,
are crying inside me
while the Saracen moon
laughs her dark laugh.

I lie alone on this bed
too large for me
in this room with a faint smell of withering violets,
lavender and dried rose petals.

Hush, little egg.
There's nothing
I can do.
Hush and die
in peace
when your counted hours
expire.

Elegy to My Father

*. . . when there is love, the widowed must stay for
the resurrection of the beloved — so that the one
who has gone is not really dead, but grows and
is created for a second time in the soul of the
living. . . .*

Carson McCullers, *The Heart is a Lonely Hunter*

Mother writes that your grave looks like a little garden now.
The primroses and the daffodils we planted in April
are blooming. We worked on your freshly-dug grave for days,
digging with cold hands for the seed in the soil,
muddy with pre-alpine rain and decomposed humanity.
She writes that she likes to sit by your grave on Sundays,
to caress the blossoms and to punish the daring weeds;
she tells you about your far-away daughter, and asks you
to keep your omniscient eye on her.

I feel your hand on my head, father.
I had to bury you to love you, father.

You were a small man, father, perhaps not even
five foot five. So, I married someone six foot four.
I thought you were a weak man, father. So,
I married someone I thought was strong.
You would walk miles to save a bus fare, father.
So, I married a spendthrift.
Now all those bus fares you saved
allow me to keep a good house and a good car.

I would sigh with impatience–my eyes
looking up to the ceiling–
when you would start reciting from *The Iliad,*
my pedantic father. Your voice
sounded so grandiloquent,
as you declamed in Greek with hieratic gestures:

> *Sing, Goddess, the anger of Peleus' son Achilleus
> and its devastation, which put pains thousandfold upon the
> Achaians . . .*

I did not understand your Greek, father. It sounded
so highfalutin, and in those days
I fed on Tennyson and the Rossettis.
I hurt you, father, when I so doggedly
refused to learn Greek.

The night you died,
you asked me to remain by your bedside.
"Because *She* is coming," you whispered to me with complicity.
I scolded you, father. I thought you were malingering.
"What is this nonsense?!" I said. "The doctor says *you're fine.*"

But She did come, that night, and I was not there, father.
You faced her alone. *My hero,* at last. At your funeral,
tears felt like icicles inside my eyelids, like the frozen
droplets spiking the pupils of the sinners in Caina,
traitors to their own kin.

After your burial, I worked on your grave for days, father,
planting seedlings and watering them
with the tears that finally melted down my cheeks.
I am learning Greek now, father. Sometimes I catch myself
declaiming your favorite passage from *The Iliad,* I also

with a stentorian voice. Of your slight body, father,
I remember only your blue eyes sparkling as you spoke
in the persona of Achilleus the hero, berating Lykaon
for cowardice toward his untimely but fated death:

> Now there is not one who can escape death, if the Gods send
> him against my hand in front of Ilion, not one
> of all the Trojans and beyond others the children of Priam.
> So, friend, you die also. Why all this clamor about it?

Yes, father, I had to bury you to learn how to love you,
you and the things you loved.

Cycle

I am my son, my mother, my father,
I am born of myself
my own flesh sucked

Lawrence Ferlinghetti

And when I cried

–bereft–

my parents said

   "Why cry
as if you didn't have
a mother and a father

still?"

My father died
meeting
Death with the enormous
eyes of a frightened bird

Now I am my mother's mother

Power and loneliness

To Sylvia Plath, Anne Sexton, Alfonsina Storni, Antonia Pozzi, Marina Tsvetayeva, Virginia Woolf, and Ingrid Jonker, An Angry Requiem

Do not feel safe. The poet remembers.
You can kill one, but another is born.
The words are written down, the deed, the date.

Czeslaw Milosz

If the best of us
want only to die,
and take their lives
yearning
for the embrace of the earth
as warm and moist
as our wombs

Then
who will be left
to carry the Pain
on muscular shoulders
for the sisters who are now
in the cradle?

We think sometimes—
when Loneliness bites our liver
with its sharp beak—
that it would be easy
to float away, new Ophelias
on a streaming bed of water lilies,
or to get ourselves to a nunnery
where the Pain is lulled
by the anesthesia of God and the Blessed Virgin.

But then
who would be left
for the non-virgins of tomorrow, for the less
courageous of today?

Don't let yourself
float away. Get thee to the rocky shore.

As the Bee Emerges

On a haiku by Basho

As the bee emerges
dizzily reluctant
from the depth
of the peony

I come up
to the blue sky again
hover above

red seas of peonies
in the uncertain joy
of the possibility of choice

II

MEDITERRANEAN POEMS

There pomegranates, quinces,
swarthy gods, uncles and cousins
emptying oil into giant jars;
and breaths from the ravine fragrant
with osier and terebinth
broom and ginger root . . .

Odysseus Elytis

Sicilian Cities

I remember them now—
emerging from flumed valleys
and parched fields hedged by prickly pears:

Cities of stone and clay
against a cloudless sky

Islands of walls and churches

Citadels of memory
       rising suddenly from crescent-shaped gulfs

the sea is calm
in halcyon days

I see them now:

Cities of light and shadow
where the Sirocco whispers in Arabic

streets of cobblestones
climbing fast toward church-pinnacled summits

windows and doors at night
like huge dark mouths

fierce balconies—lion heads
      support them—empty:
who waters the carnations?

Dried yellow moss
on terra-cotta rooftops:

ravens and swallows
circle darkly above them.

My cities.

Cities of saints and beggars

Cities of silence startled by sudden noise

Cities of Mary Magdalens — dark-veiled —
furtively crossing lanes
where grass grows pertinacious
in cracks and crevices . . .

Was it yesterday?
   There, out at sea,
   large ships sailed away,
   pennons rippling in the breeze,
     masts, stays and rigging
       growing smaller in the distance.
   They all wore a cross on their sails:
   Crusaders bound for Ultramar.

Sicilian cities.

We still sail away from them,
for other shores, for other sorrows.

But we remember them always
from afar.

Sicilian cities.

Time appears not to touch them.

Islanders

It takes a special talent to be an islander,
a talent you acquire
by being born on one.
Islands are not for everyone;
they are for those
who know that limits are to be trespassed,
that the sea encircles and encloses,
but that it also connects.
Islands are fragments
of ancient mountaintops.
They contain
the pattern of the universe.
Islands still remember
when the Gods walked with men.
On an island
you can get to know a place totally,
sandbars and reefs,
rivers and woods, tangles of wildflowers, cattails
and marsh birds, people
and the state of their soul:
for on an island
the soul is naked.
Islands are unexpected
places, hard to reach, though at times
near one another, like the archipelago
of the eleven thousand virgins.
When you step on an island,
the gates close behind you.
You become one
of the silent, secret sort.
When the boat leaves,

some feel stranded, abandoned.
I feel delivered. I return to the roots
of my own being.
For I was born on an island.
An island with three corners.

The Carob Tree

We always leave
a part of ourselves
behind us.

I know I shall not find it;
and yet I am compelled
to go looking for it—
for the spot where it once stood—
so that my eyes will at last
believe that things have changed.
Time has passed, three whole lusters,
since we sauntered up,
as children, in the night's silence
broken only by our laughter;
we climbed the hill
to the huge carob tree.

We sat at its foot, on a bed of dry grass: the tree
hovered over us with its rustling
arms, protecting us from the fear
our own tales created.
We felt like heroes
who had braved Scylla and Charybdis, intrepid
explorers of the dark . . .

The lights dimly shining
down there
in the town—
belonged to those who never dared, never climbed,
never searched. We knew
we were different:

we were the Argonauts
of a town without sea.
We turned the night
and the thick grass into an ocean,
our bare feet
into ship-bows.

They tell me it no longer
exists—the old carob tree—
that a large house now stands in its place,
surrounded
by a cluster of new buildings.

They say there,
up the hill,
it's no longer
unexplored no-man's-land
in the middle
of imagined rough waves.

The town itself
has climbed up the hill,
claiming it with cement.

I know I shall not find it.
And yet I must go see—
see if it's there.

Atlantis

On the Greek island of Santorini

Standing
        on the tip of
                Atlantis

I question
        the crisp surface

Where the sea is
                bluest

I see

tall cities and
        towers and
                walls and
wide cobblestone roads

chariots carrying
        amphoras and
                vases

women
        covered with hand-hammered
                glistening gold

        reposing
                soft-cushioned in the
                        sand

lissome skeletons
    stretching out in the
            endless
    yawn of death

bones exquisite

    wide
    lipless smiles
            at the tickle of
    small fish

Coins and
iron tripods
    and cooking pots
            overturned
and blacksmith's tools
        rusting
among dark algae

I am standing
        on the brink
of an infinite
        cemetery

Joyous
I hear calling
the voice of the wind

Breakup in Venice

Look. It's August in Venice and we are supposed to be
like honeymooners, but we are really breaking up.
We both know it, but neither of us
will fess up to it.

We stare at the canals at sunset,
when they reflect
both the sun and the moon.
The lamplight shines
on a carnation fallen off a gondola,
and on a plastic doll
floating face up with eyes wide-open
under white laundry hung out to dry.

Look. The city turns red
before being suddenly engulfed
by a Turner-like greenish brown—
as the noise of the day
quiets down in the shimmer of night.
Ominous looms
the roof of the Piombi
from which Casanova escaped—if one is to believe him.
Can anyone escape? I know you are trying
to escape from me. Will I let you?

From the lit window of a closed store,
some masks stare at us: a sad Harlequin and a perky Colombina
appear to converse in silence.

In this town,
which is dying a glorious death,
plaster, bricks and foundations
are slowly eroded
by the soothing waters.

The end is coming,
so soon,
so gently.

The First Winter after the War

That winter—
my first winter in the city—
I saw snow
          and touched ice
                    for the first time
as we moved North
leaving the island
          and the summer behind us

I learnt to keep quiet
to draw faces on foggy windowpanes, to eat icicles

For the first time
I saw the world through a window
(down South
we just went outside)

I learned
things had to be bought–not just
picked from the fields–
You had to pay
even for one chestnut

Here people did not smile
but they kept busy:
they went out
even in the cold storm.
I could see them from my post at the window
all grey in the grey street
          under a grey sky.

That winter
I learned silence
         I learned cold
     I learned hunger

That winter
I stopped crying

I was only three

Baroque Churches

Pink and plump was the flesh chastised and exhalted in those vast
    churches

where from high frescoed ceilings hung garlands of cherubs

where the scent of white lilies stunned like a love filter

where plaster saints lurched in niches flanked by bloody ex-votoes

where behind carved confessionals

old prelates listened to whispered *mea culpas*

where time moved slowly minute by minute like beads of old
    rosary chains

The contemplation of sin and the mortification of the body

moved us to obsess

on that very young flesh we were taught to ignore,

while we lit candles in front of the lissome limbs of the martyrs:

Saint Sebastian studded with arrows,

his loins barely veiled by a diaphanous cloth,

his white skin enlivened by droplets of red blood—

as red as the carnation a lover furtively tosses

to his beloved

There Were . . .

There were baptisms and marriages,
and deaths and wakes, and virgins dreaming of fulfillment,
and married women waiting for the joys promised them.
There were long processions on saint days,
and nights when the sky was lit up by fireworks.

There was the safety of ancestral houses
built with thick walls; and, on the threshold,
there were old women reciting the rosary,
holding the brown beads in their bony hands.
And there were children sitting under walls
hot with the dog-days' sun,
teasing lizards.

There were mothers in the shade of fig trees
nursing infants who bit their nipples laughing:
the whiteness of their breasts
offset their dark tresses.
And against the cracked walls
exploded the petals of red bougainvilleas,
and the curly heads of the lantana bushes
beside cascades of golden
laburnum. They grew, it seems, with no water.
They grew
in spite of everything.

Now, I remember it all,
and build a shrine to my nostalgia.
I sit next to my grandfather's picture,
as I then sat by the potted creeper,
teasing lizards.

Of that world,

I'm the last
of the
chroniclers.

III

PERSONAE

Comprendo
que el comprador de mitos
y misterios
entre
en mi casa de odas,
hecha con adobe y madera,
y odie
los utensilios,
los retratos
de padre y madre y patria
en las paredes
la sencillez
del pan
y del salero.
Pero así es la casa de mis odas.

Pablo Neruda

On Pollaiolo's Portrait of a Renaissance Woman

Simple and noble your long-necked profile
stares calmly into spaces
visible to you only. You would be perfect
symmetry, if the pendant
of your gemmed necklace were not
slightly askew.

Pearls and gold ribbons
gently hold your blond hair
at the back of your exquisitely molded
head, in intricate designs.

Only your ears
are covered with a diaphanous
shell of lace, as if to shield you
from the noise of the world.

O nameless maiden,
forever unperturbed,
you keep on looking
into your hidden space.

Your lips are slightly tight
as if you knew a secret
and could not tell it.

Artemis

There is a time in every woman's life when she wants to belong
only to herself: she then becomes Artemis.

My companions are the cypress and the fir; my solace
the crocus and the cyclamen:
they spring up from my footprints.

I am Artemis.
I walk alone
on paths uncharted.
I love the woods
and the wild chase over the mountains.
I have rough hands and delicate feet.

I am the sovereign
of all that is wild and solitary.
The storm abates
when I charm it.

Aphrodite cannot stir my heart. My beauty
is only for myself. No one can touch me.
I long for no one.
I am as cold as the moon,
as mysterious as the deep recesses of the earth.

I love the whisper of brooks
and the roar of waterfalls.
I sleep lulled
by the rustling of leaves.
I sleep alone
like a child or an old woman.

Silence is music to me.
I hear notes
in the terse air.

I am fierce.
I am merciful.
I am undisturbed.

Cassandra

On the anniversary of the Persian Gulf War

Every age has its Trojan War.

Odysseus Elytis

Forgotten people
recognize one another.
Many know about me.

Willows grew in profusion
by the Scamander.
There I went gathering
supple willow rods.

I longed for love
unbearably.
But I could not reach out for it:
love is not for prophets.
Love is not for seers.
They are born to give it,
not to receive it.

During the years of war
we forgot how and why it all started:
whatever it was, it was just a pretext, anyway.
War starts as a game.
We did not think of *why* any longer,
we thought only of *when* it would end.

On the other side,
there were those I knew were fated to win:
strangers gutted by homesickness,
the way we were gutted
by hopelessness.

And my prophecies . . . unheeded.
Like dreams, they were insoluble tangles.

Was I to repeat them again and again?
Men hated me for that.
They avoided me as if I were armed.
For prophecy is like a bow: it shoots
sharp darts that wound.
There were gaps
in time. Time was still
as I once more
prophesied what lay already
outside the Scaean gates.

I wanted to go to Greece,
unaware of what I was looking for:
like all wanderers,
I was looking for something.
Something was beckoning to me: the fulfillment.
To the house of Atreus,
they took me captive.
With my second sight,
I sensed death
within the door:
Agamemnon's and mine.

So, I made my way into death, gently,
as a ship into deep waters,
with the indifference of the celestials.
I released
the cords that bound me to Life.
For we do not die
unless we want to die.

I did not wish
the gift of prophecy: for who wants
to recollect the future
as if it were the past?
Glimpses of the future
encircled me, gnawed at me
as the past gnaws at a bad conscience.

I saw the slaughter continue
bloody, senseless.
year after year,
century after century, millennium after millennium.
I saw new weapons spitting fire from the sky,
new wounds, new diseases,
and fire raining down from the clouds,
and tall mushrooms of smoke
obfuscating
the sun and the moon.
I saw it all
but I could not stop it.
I told them,
but they would not listen.

I was Cassandra.
The seer.
The scorned.
The unbelieved.

In me
there was something of
everyone.
We all know,
if we want to know.
But knowledge is the hardest thing.
Harder than death.

Persephone Writes to Demeter from Hades

It was not a rape, mother.
I went of my own free will.
And it was not by accident
that I ate the pomegranate seeds.

I longed for Hades, its shade, its dark
tranquillity.
Your love, mother,
scorched and burned me
as the dog-days' sun
parches the earth in August.
Love can be
as deadly as hate . . .
Do you know that, mother,
you who love me so much?

With you, I was always
in the light,
always blinded
by brightness.
I longed to be left alone,
in a corner, like a forgotten thing.
Always living in the light is hard, mother.
My eyes needed rest
from the profusion of gold
you sow on earth. It was all too much, mother,
too much light,
too many cicadas and crickets singing on the fig trees,
too many
golden spears of wheat in the fields.

Don't weep for me, mother.
I will be with you again in Spring,
when I will make the daffodils and the crocus bloom.

I'll made the hyacinth
fill the valley with fragrance,
the aloof flower of the agave
will soar again over fields of red poppies.
And I will be with you
during the time of harvest
when you bestow
your goodwill on the earth.
But after that,
I'll return
to my shadowy kingdom.

The darkness of Hades
is soothing to me, mother.
There, I do not have to shine,
nor dance, nor smile, nor produce flowers
and rainbows and soft zephyrs
to stir the buds.

There I can just rest
in halls cushioned
with grey softness,
in the chiaroscuro
of the winter months . . .

No, it was not rape,
dear mother.
Nor was it by accident
that I ate the pomegranate seeds.

The Penelope Triptych

Penelope in the First Decade

Once before
over
a decade ago

I sat home
weaving my patient web
while you, Odysseus
exultant

were buffeted from shore to shore
crossed
the windy Cyclades
escaped
one-eyed Polyphemus
and the white
arms of Circe

This time

I shall not at night unravel
the weft
woven in the sunlight
It is taking shape
color and meaning
from my wordless anguish

My web is screaming
to the beholder
like Philomel's ripped tongue,

and I'll let it scream
in the sunlight

Penelope in the Second Decade

They all sailed forth
to their distant homes
in battered ships
loaded with loot and dreams
of peaceful times ahead

Menelaus and Helen
reconciled
by her second betrayal . . .
Agamemnon blind
to his fateful homecoming

Only Odysseus
for one more decade
roamed the wide seas—
his childlike soul still thirsty
for pain and wonder

his strength in the awareness
that I, Penelope,
as receptive as the Ionian sea

sat, weaving
year after year

in my patience,
stronger than him

Penelope in the Third Decade

It was all a story, that about Fate
and the wrath of the Gods. The truth is, I bored him.
And as for me, I desired him to leave
as much as he desired it. He could never be still. Barely
had he returned than he started talking
about his next journey.
I did not mind: nobody is abandoned
who does not want to be, as well know the wives
of soldiers, sailors and of traveling merchants.

For many years, I lived by myself,
for nothing pleased me better
than to sleep alone, to own my body.
All called me chaste, praised my fidelity. But I was not
faithful to *him*. I was faithful to *myself*.
I wove and unraveled, I twisted
threads of many colors into wondrous shapes
—and then, I unraveled them all.

> *We all make our fate, Odysseus, I thought,*
> *and you made yours of wanderer and adventurer.*
> *And I made mine of stable and prudent queen.*
> *We all make our fate, then blame the gods for it.*
> *Without knowing it, we had been well-paired:*
> *you, who always wanted to roam,*
> *and I, who always wanted to stay —*
> *we both had our freedom.*

It pleased him to think that I waited for him with longing.
But I waited, if you can call it that, calmly,
enjoying life day by day: I had a child, a household,
a storeroom with *pithoi* filled with oil and grain,

an orchard with fig trees and pomegranates,
sweet hills covered with purple grapevines,
a garden where blue agapanthus seemed to soar.

A good life.
I understood that what is far is as near as near,
and near is as far as far,
and that no journey can be enjoyed
without the thought of the return.

And who is the hero? The one who departs? The one who stays?
Ultimately, they end up at the same place — and often,
the one who stayed has traveled
farther than the wanderer . . .
an inward journey.

It surprised him that I did not recognize him at first.
Recognize him I did, but I wanted to buy time.
He told me about the Nymph and the Sorceress,
how they had wanted him,
how they had tried to detain him. . . .
Why did he tell me? I did not
ask. I did not care.
Again, I surrendered myself to him,
knowing that it would not be for long.

And the cycle began again. He left
on another adventure. This time,
never to come back.
It did not sadden me, for I was navigating
the seas of *my own* mind.

I was traveling
inside myself,
deeper and deeper . . .
until I found
what I had been looking for:
and what that is,
I will never tell
anyone.

Anna Comnena Starts to Write the *Alexiad*

Time, in its irresistible flow,
carries away all things created
to drown them in obscurity. Thus, from the darkness,
Time brings events to their birth, and then
wraps them again in the black night.
Against this destruction,
History forms a strong bulwark, securing
and binding facts together, preventing them
from slipping into oblivion.

I, Anna Comnena,
daughter
of two royal personages,
recognize this fact. I was born
of Alexius and Irene. I was born
and bred in the purple.
I was not ignorant of letters. I pursued
my Greek studies to the highest degree.
I studied Plato and Aristotle with care.
I was not unschooled in rhetoric.

I intend now
to record the deeds of my father Alexius,
so that they be not swept away
by a sea of forgetfulness.
I am going to relate these deeds
not to show off my proficiency in letters,
but so that they will be known
to future generations: for even the greatest exploits
are swallowed by silence,

if they are not preserved
by the written word.

I have been aware of danger
since my birth. Fortune was not kind to me,
unless you count as kindness
to have given me imperial parents.
All my life has been a series
of storms and revolutions, of rivers
and streams of misfortunes.
Now it is winding down. As I write this,
I know that my life has not been lived in vain,
nor have the lives of those who lived before me,
and gave me life.

To them,
and to myself,
I build this monument.

The Poem Talks to the Poet

For Lawrence Ferlinghetti

*The Aztecs believed that poems reside in heaven and that poets
could make them rain down with prayer and chant.*

Make room for me!

From the mansions of the gods
I will rain down on you
soft and sweet as summer dew

Set your house in order
Perfume every room with copal

Get ready for me
as a bride awaiting her groom

Lay out your best clothing
your rattles and your feathers

Adorn yourself
with jade and turquoise

Set your heart at peace

I will come

You will find the words
to greet me

Joyously I will come
to say
what is in your heart

IV

STILL LIFE WITH SEASHELLS

Isole che ho abitato
verdi su mari immobili

D'alghe sparse, di fossili marini
le spiagge ove corrono in amore
cavalli di luna e di vulcani.

Salvatore Quasimodo

Still Life with Seashells

To a sea-lover from a sea-lover

Across the Atlantic I am sending you a bundle of seashells.
Some met my fingers as I was sifting the sand on a beach
on Martha's Vineyard, others I found in a store, shipped
from oriental seashores.

I want to speak to you with the voice of the sea. Hold them,
one by one, against your ear: they are the mouths of the sea.
Through their opening, it whispers stories and legends,
it reveals the maps of sunken treasures, it echoes
the songs of long-haired sirens
swimming gracefully between the masts of shipwrecked vessels.

Before sending them, I place them on a platter
and meditate upon their shapes and colors: once
they were living animals too, underneath their variegated
carapaces, covering up, like human beings, soft under-
bellies and weakness.
Some are striped like zebras,
some dotted black like printed newspaper,
and some purple, like Tyrian cloth. One looks
like a scorpion, with long sharp prongs and a pointed stinger,
but underneath it is rosy and delicate, so vulnerable.
There are clams and limpet shells also, so round,
so smooth. And here is a sand dollar, white, brittle, how
could it withstand the furious waves? It opened up little holes,
so as not to offer resistance. And look, another shell, the turbo,
has the pointed shape of a Circassian tent, or the coil
of a Janissary's turban; this one looks like a drill, or a spindle,

sharp and elongated; and yet another has the shape
of an olive, long and green.

All of them have stories to tell, if you listen.
When they had their soft bodies, they used to travel slowly
on the bottom of the sea. They have seen immense jungles of kelp
and forests of sunken masts, with long-armed plants
streaming from them. They have caressed gently
the levigated skeletons of ancient
mariners claimed by the sea-gods, lulled in their
eternal repose in beds of luminescent sand.

They moved on to shores of enchanted islands, where they rested
under palm trees, undisturbed by human presence.
And then they were caught by whirlwinds,
by the immense cataclysms that the sea uses
to activate life, to churn it up, to redistribute it
to all the corners of the earth. Or they ended up
where the hand of a boy gathered them to sell
to those who love the sea, and who long for its fluid peace.

The Poet's Nasturtiums

For Giuseppe Conte

I planted nasturtiums because you wrote about them.
I saw them in your poems first: bright, profuse,
glorious with shades of orange, amaranth,
garnet-red and maize-yellow, flowers suited
to make garlands for the foreheads of the Gods.

One day I planted the large seeds in the soil; a few days later
the stems appeared, thin, tall,
topped with shield-like leaves
that turned around, following the light like sunflowers.
Soon they were growing into vines,
graceful lianas twisting and coiling
like green serpents in a convoluted ascent.
They grew faster than ivy, scaling the stone wall.

They make me think of you, and of a Matisse painting
where they overflow from round vessels,
while lithe figures dance in the background
and goldfish swim in a glass bowl.
They make me think of you, of where
you have seen them, in your far-away land,
which is also my land.

Their smell is pungent—my nose twists if I get too close.
They will last all summer and into the fall,
tendrils weaving more and more complex patterns—
till the flowers form a thick carpet of lustrous hues.

They are in my garden but they belong to you.
They were planted in your pages first—
and there I saw them with my mind's eye.
And although I have never met you,
I see you when I look at them.

The Trip We Never Took

During the trip we never took, we sailed across the Aegean,
where frequently an island would appear, topped
with whitewashed houses, flat-roofed, scattered on steep slopes
like grazing sheep. Here and there, the blue top of a white church
would soar like a holy balloon.
Winds of the Cyclades! During that voyage,
they touched our skin with ardor, regaling us
with fragrances of jasmine and of seashells.

During the trip we never took, we sailed down
the Dalmatian coastline, skirting islets covered with seaweed,
shining like emeralds in the sun, leeward sails
filled with strong gusts of wind. We sighted cities and villages
with unknown names, in search of a harbor
we recognized although we had never seen it.

During the trip we never took, we walked
along flat sandy beaches, sweet to the feet, past little coves
crowned with palm trees leaning on turquoise water.
During the trip we never took, we picked
imaginary seashells I'm holding now in my hands.

During the trip we never took, we saw people with eyes
of all hues, skins of all shades, speaking languages
with different, sonorous sounds. We strolled down Gothic lanes,
discovering new sights around each corner; we leaned over
canals and riverbanks, listening to the water
whisper to us. We pushed through jungles, climbed steep pyramids
soaring high, overlooking tropical tangle, until we reached
the sacrificial chamber at the top—and there we paused,
breathless, feeling the spirits of the past.

During the trip we never took, we were happy and carefree,
laughing in the breeze, running and playing like children, intent
on exploring the world around us, to show
each other the little marvels we had discovered.

During the trip we never took
we were happy together.

On A Few Japanese Prints

Kiyonaga

The two lovers meet
under a flowering tree—
In her hand a fan

Utamaru

A small-faced servant
hides behind the courtesan
who does not see her

Kiyomitsu

Sweet autumn evening:
Three dancers before a screen
move, their robes flouncing

Harunobu

Gently bending down
a maid on a mountain path
feeds two white cranes

Open kimono
by the sunny veranda
reveals tender breasts

Koryusai

Intent, majestic,
the courtesan reads of love
Her servants play cards

Montezuma Sends His Messengers to Cortés

It was the year 13-Rabbit.
After his messengers went to talk to the Gods,
Montezuma could neither eat nor sleep.
The great *tlatoani* said to himself:
"If Quetzalcoatl has returned
as he promised when he departed many *katúns* ago,
nothing will comfort me, nothing will give me pleasure.
The end that the portents foreshadowed is here.
My heart suffers and burns as if it were drowned in spices."

When the messengers returned from the sea,
Montezuma went to see them at the House of the Serpent.
He had war prisoners painted with chalk,
their hearts torn out with obsidian knives,
and the messengers were sprinkled with sacrificial blood,
for they had completed their mission. One by one,
they reported.

The first messenger said: "The Gods came over the sea,
floating in wooden houses. On earth
they are carried by large stags, as tall
as the roof of a house."

The second messenger said: "The Gods are completely covered,
but we could see their faces. Their skin is white.
Most of them have hair the color of maize
shining in the sun."

The third messenger said: "Their arms are made of iron,
their clothes are made of iron,
their bows are made of iron, their shields and spears

also made of iron.
The Gods are made of iron."

The fourth messenger said: "The Gods want gold, a lot of gold.
They say they have an ailment,
an ailment only gold can cure."

The last messenger said: "The Gods have a magic weapon.
It roars. It rains fire. From its entrails,
it spits out stone balls. From afar,
it can split open a mountain and mangle people's limbs."

When Montezuma heard this, his heart was sore
as if pierced by the maguey thorn.
He was vanquished from within.

He resigned himself.
The prophecy was fulfilled.
There was nothing that he could do now
but to let it unfold
to the end.

The Awakening of the Apple Tree

The tree up there—at the top of my garden,
                              just above the little pond
the tree that for many years, every spring
blossomed but never produced fruit—

is suddenly loaded with hard
little green apples that weigh down its branches
spinning playfully in the wind by their stems.

That tree—
I did not even know it was an apple tree.

Thus a woman
who has been barren for a long time,
suddenly swells in pregnancy, bears a child.

Thus a poet
who has not sung for a long time,
suddenly bursts into song.

What sudden stirrings of dark forces—
what powerful urges to bud,
what mysterious
deadline in nature's timetable

have brought forth such a miracle?

Simply,

it was time.

V

THE RETURN

"My old friend, what are you looking for?
After years abroad, you've come back
with images you've nourished
under foreign skies
far from your own country."

"I'm looking for my old garden;
the trees come to my waist
and the hills resemble terraces
yet as a child
I used to play on the grass
under great shadows
and I would run for hours
breathless over the slopes."

George Seferis

The Storm Petrel

This poem came to me after I translated Diane di Prima's "Rant" into Italian; it is therefore dedicated to her.

I was always
a storm petrel

I seek deserted islets
nesting
in chinks in the rocks

I set off
at the first
      violent
gusts of wind

I come alive
with the darkening of the shadows
      when the rain riots
           in the woods

I like being
in the storm's eye: there I find
the stillness of halcyon days.

Most birds
sleep in soft-cushioned nests.
I sleep
on the wind.

I wanted to know
how vast the world really is,
the true shape of islands,
the taste of the dew
in clearings rimmed with moonlight,
the rustling of sails
      listing to open sea
            as taut as archers' bows.
I wanted to see
the clouds from above
as soft as sea foam.
I wanted to feel
the presence of water
down below.

I am more eloquent
when I do not speak.
My silence
is as haunting as the last
      cry
            across the water

I am in good terms
with the Sun and the Moon.

I TELL YOU

There is more danger
in a closed mind
than in a storm or an earthquake.

I TELL YOU

The world truly is inexhaustible.

Do not stand still.

Nothing is as wonderful
as being on the brink.

Eating Alone at a Chinese Restaurant

For Luigi Fontanella

My chopsticks are inlaid with graceful designs,
but I ask for a fork.
They have seated me at a small table in the back,
toward the kitchen. I hear voices coming
from behind a screen.
I do not know whether they are joking or quarreling.
The sounds are lilting, the words thick and fast.
What can they be saying?
I cannot see the speakers. Behind the screen,
they live in a world of their own.
Maybe they are thinking of their far-away country
while shelling pea pods and cutting water chestnuts.

On the wall hangs a large painting
of a river flowing through steep gorges laced with waterfalls . . .
The mountaintops disappear in ringlets of clouds
into heavens of Taoist gods. A few houses and pagodas
are scattered on the slopes.
At the river mouth, a few ships sail away.

The voices in the kitchen are still talking.
What are they saying? Are they happy, or are they speaking
of loneliness?

My fortune cookie says:

YOU WILL TRAVEL FAR AND WIDE

I too come from a far-away country.

The Wanderer

Inspired by a pre-Socratic fragment

Long voyages
and weary wanderings

sailing at night
amidst
tumultuous waves

Living abroad

far from home

Working and toiling
      to collect what
            cannot be carried home

And all
      for
         what?

How Could They?

How could my ancestors leave those cities—
those cities of limestone and sun,
of Baroque intricacies in the wrought-iron balconies,
and walls with caper plants
blooming in the cracks—
How could they allow
the silence to reclaim them?

Ships floated away from the coast
as on wide wings:
my people
scattered to the four directions—
as when the milkweed pod splits
flinging
white fluff to the winds.

As for me,
I do not know why I went away.
I was not moved by need.
I do not even know
if it was my heart's desire:
Fate and man's will
are two different things.

Now,
I look at the stars and I think of my land,
the land of the cactus people.
The same stars shine there,
the same moon.

My land, I think of you.

In my thoughts,
I caress you with flowers.

Oranges from Ancient Orchards

On that hill
we used to call mountain,
there was a sharp odor
of marjoram and wild mint.

I have walked your path today,
grandfather, in memory of you.
I stopped, as we did then,
in the shade of a pomegranate.

We abandoned the lands of the South.
We left behind those lands
where the children's eyes are sad,
where the winds reach out from North Africa.

Now the Southwind leads me
through this deserted town.
Here I was nourished with honey and figs,
in these sun-baked streets
flanked by sandstone and prickly pears.

I taste oranges
stolen from ancient orchards.

The moon sets
down the throats of barking dogs.

My cry
will rise at dawn
from a cradle
of deep furrows:
I will sing to the burning sun.

Here, now, in the dust,
I write down these lines.
If I could, like a bird in flight,
I would trace my words
in the air.

The Return

At night I look at the stars—
                    the Chaldean stars.

Under the tessellated sky
                    so much land—nothing but land—
trees of great shade   bushes and woods
            a splendor of spears
                        indigo and gold
                            in the moonlight.

From this hemisphere
I have watched portents in the sky
                    eclipses biting at the sun
In the middle of the moon
            white sails that lull in water—
mountains that are no mountains.

Destiny has prodded me in all directions
since I came forth from my mother's womb—

I parted with my land for a while,
so that I would not be parted forever.

For sheafs of years
I have sifted the ashes of foreign lands.

Now my song
                pierces like a knife:
I am one of the rememberers.

We all come from somewhere
and there we must return.

The sky pales: it is time.
I shall return to my land.

There is my ziggurat.

The Talatat

My poems will not change the world
but they will tell I existed.
I write
so that those after me will know
I was born, I breathed, I loved,
I felt joy, I felt pain.

I have suffered through
bitter winters and sung
for many springs.
Now it is time to pause,
to document.

As I write I am etching
my story in a long-lasting
limestone talatat.
It will survive.
Thus I assuage
the fear of dying.

I have not given birth
to a child.
But I write this.

Envoi

I leave this book as a time capsule.
It's all here, there is little that I've left out.
Here, it says I was born on Persephone's island,
but that I was taken as a little girl to the Northern mists.
That I was born at a time of war, and fought against war all my life.
That I left home early to explore the world,
that I was transplanted many times,
and felt rootless — until I found roots within myself.
And here it says that I loved, and more than one time,
and that every time it tore me apart.
That I was married and divorced, and divorce scarred me deeply,
and I will carry the scar to my dying day.
That children did not come to me for reasons I cannot disclose
because they were not disclosed to me.
That I loved flowers and beautiful things beyond my means,
and seashells of all shapes and music with minor chords.
That I loved boats and ships and caiques, white sails on the bay,
and bright spinnakers billowing in the wind.
That I loved to travel, but that I always yearned
for the place where I was born.
That I was a loner, who liked to stay awake when others slept.
That I had a lot more than other women have, and a lot less.
That I loved the Moon more than the Sun.
That I was afraid of death and its destruction,
and that I wrote poems to keep part of me alive.
That I want to return full circle to the slopes of my volcano,
to a small town where I will tell dark-eyed children
stories of the places I visited.
That of all things, I loved the Written Word best.
There it's where it all started,
and where it will all end.

END NOTES

BURMESE RECOLLECTIONS
Pagan, in Burma, lies Southwest of Mandalay on the Irrawaddy River. Until 1298, it was the ancient capital of the Burmese kingdom. Presently, it is only a village, but hundreds of pagodas and temples in various stages of decay can be seen throughout the jungle around the village. *That Byinnyu, Ananda*: Large temples. *Longyi*: Ankle-length skirt worn by the Burmese. *Stupa:* Votive building with a conic shape in which a treasure dedicated to a divinity is often hidden.

BREAKUP IN VENICE
The *Piombi*, the Venetian jail, was thus named for its lead roofs. Casanova claimed to have escaped from it.

BAROQUE CHURCHES
In Catholic churches, one can often see *ex-votoes*, offerings presented to saints or to Jesus as thanks for special favors received. They can be of precious metals, and often in the shapes of healed body parts: feet, hearts, eyes, etc.

ELEGY TO MY FATHER
Dante, in his *Inferno*, places the traitors to their own kin in Caina,the lowest circle of hell, a frozen pit, since treason is a cold-blooded sin.

ON POLLAIOLO'S PORTRAIT OF A RENAISSANCE WOMAN
This famous portrait by Renaissance painter Pollaiolo can be seen at the Poldi Pezzoli Museum in Milan.

ANNA COMMENA STARTS TO WRITE THE *ALEXIAD*
This poem was inspired by the Prologue to the *Alexiad*. Anna Comnena, born in 1083, is the first known woman historian. She recorded the deeds of her father Alexius I Comnenus of the Byzantine Comneni family, and the events around the First Crusade to Constantinople.

MONTEZUMA SENDS HIS MESSENGERS TO CORTÉS
This poem was inspired by Aztec documents in Nahúatl reported by Fray Bernardino de Sahagún in his *Historia général de las cosas de*

Nueva España, in the *Codex Florentino*.

Line 5: Quetzalcoatl was an Aztec God that had disappeared, vowing to return. The appearance of the Spaniards, floating in boats, riding the horse — an animal never seen before — and carrying "magic" weapons, convinced the Aztecs of their god-like status.

THE TALATAT

Talatat: Stone in which were recorded the exploits of ancient kings and warriors.

About *The Moon and the Island*

Laura Stortoni or Anna Stortoni? Poets with three names, poetesses with three names, have always been signs of genteel suburban consciousness to me, but Laura or Anna isn't in that league in poems of hers like "To Sylvia Plath, Anne Sexton, Alfonsina Storni, Antonia Pozzi, Marina Tsvetayeva, Virginia Woolf, and Ingrid Jonker: An Angry Requiem." It is in the same class as the poets she names in the title. . . . . Laura Stortoni's poetry hovers between her lost world and our new one, her voice echoing both.

Lawrence Ferlinghetti
Poet, Painter

These poems blend a bright, rich, sensual Mediterranean vitality with the austere joy of a woman's search for self in the solitude of alienation from lover and from native country. The range of emotions, from exaltation to terror, takes on the topographical quality of a landscape through which one follows the author on a personal, historical, mythological journey toward revelations and insights, never facile, always earned, that rise up like angels—or dragons—at each turn of the trail or beyond the crest of each hill.

Stephen Meats
Poet, Poetry Editor, *The Midwest Quarterly*

Laura Stortoni gives us lyrical, sensuous poems that shape a world rooted in the dailiness of one woman's life, yet connected to the lives of all people by myth and dream. Passionate and moving, imagistic and specific, these poems are poems of loss and survival and celebration.

Maria Mazziotti Gillan
Poet, Director, Passaic Poetry Center; Editor, *The Paterson Literary Review*

The voice speaking in Laura Stortoni's poetry is a voice that knows a thousand tones and a thousand spells: now it is foreign, wrenched away from the silence with love and pain; now it is near, domestic, like the voice of a friend one has always known; now it is fresh, captivating, like the voice of a friend just met. But it also knows how to be deep and mysterious, how to show the mythic and the ritual elements contained in every word that really counts.

Some are poems in which a voice speaks with everyday tones: once, alone at the table of a Chinese restaurant, the poet enters in a revealing communion with other voices, not knowing whether they are joking or whispering in the back kitchen: another time, she stages the bitter, ironic comedy of the first Thanksgiving after her divorce. But there are many other poems in which the poet is at the same time a woman of our times and a woman of myth: the voice of the present and the voice of the archetypes strangely united. Here are Artemis, Cassandra, Penelope, Persephone: the latter addresses Demeter with the words of a daughter who knows the meaning of escape, of challenge, of the voluntary journey among the shadows.

The Moon and the Island is a book that deeply moved me, a book alive, unmistakable, new and ancient, American and European, melancholic and happy: a proof, if one needs one, of the cathartic value of the light and absolute power of poetry.

Giuseppe Conte
Poet, novelist, playwright, critic

. . . . . A propos of the poems set in Sicily, I was struck by the fact that the poet renders images and ideas without nostalgic banality . . . Laura Stortoni's experience is always concrete, sensual, immediate, without rhetoric. Thus, it deepens rather then mortifies. "A Borrowed Tongue," in this non-nostalgic context, is very strong. I like "There Were. . ." very much for its concreteness and for its ending: "I am only / one of the chroniclers." There is an absolute need of such chroniclers in poetry, in life stories.

In "The Carob-Tree" and in "Sicilian Cities," the poet preserves myths in a concrete form. Thus, she transcends the suicide described in the poem to Plath, Sexton, Woolf, *et al.* Stortoni's voice emerges as a woman's presence important in American? Italian? poetry, the category does not matter. As Artemis? In Venice? Anywhere!

Everything considered, it is poetry that emerges through the eyes, and a voice that makes a deep impression.

Justin Vitiello
Professor, poet, critic.

Order Form

This book can be ordered through:

HESPERIA PRESS:
P.O. Box 9246
Berkeley, CA 94709
Phone: (510) 644-8259
Fax: (510) 644-2109

SMALL PRESS DISTRIBUTION
1341 Seventh Street
Berkeley, CA 94710
Phone: (510) 524-1668
Fax: (510) 524-0852

Please send me _____ copy (copies) of *The Moon and the Island* at:

Name: _____

Address:_____

City:_____ State:_____ Zip:_____ ____

Telephone: (____)_____; Fax: (____)_____

Cost:
$13.00 per copy

Sales Tax:
Please add $1.07 California Sales tax.

Shipping:
Add $3.00 for the first book and $1.25 for each additional. (Surface shipping may take three to four weeks).

Payment:

❑   Check

❑   Money Order